PINK THUNDER

Pink Thunder
by Michael Zapruder

Black Ocean
Boston · New York · Chicago

Black Ocean
P.O. Box 52030
Boston, MA 02205
blackocean.org

Cover design by Tony Calzaretta
Book design by Janaka Stucky
Illustrations by Arrington de Dionyso

ISBN 978-0-9844752-6-1

Cataloging in Publication data
available at the Library of Congress

FIRST EDITION

Introduction

This book / album / sculpture / scroll / stone tablet / petroglyph that you hold in your hand is ostensibly the setting of twenty-two contemporary poems to music, but it is also much, much more.

Pink Thunder is an elegantly curated anthology representing a vibrant movement in modern poetry. Michael Zapruder has collected a group of poems that illuminates a common aesthetic among friends and co-conspirators. These are poets who understand that the big grabs—Love, Family, Confession, Death—can no longer be approached directly in a convincing way. Today's audience is too savvy, too wary of manipulation and sentimentality. These poems instead stake their foundation on the minutiae of accidental revelation, trusting the details of life to point out the bigger picture.

Pink Thunder is an art show. Understanding that the possibilities raised by the project allowed for novel discovery, Zapruder envisioned a new medium for people to encounter this music. He constructed his sculptural portmanteaus—found objects incorporating hidden digital music players, a headphone jack, and an enticing red playback button.

Only a few people get the pleasure of encountering one of the portmanteaus, though. And if we want to engage with the work repeatedly, which the work itself both demands and rewards, then it requires a slightly more practical form of dissemination. So (as you obviously know), *Pink Thunder* is also a book. A gorgeous, illustrated, and hand-lettered document lush and sensual enough to pair with the rich, textured, sumptuously arranged music on the accompanying CD.

The songs on *Pink Thunder* bridge the gap between art song and popular song. Rather than sacrificing the integrity of both genres, Zapruder has managed to cherry pick the best elements of "high art" and "popular culture" to create songs that transcend the limitations of either. What better way to set poetry that deftly straddles the line between literary virtuosity and gutter slang, heartbreak and slapstick, the sacred and the profane?

Art song lovers will recognize the overt "programmatic" relationship of the music sonically describing or enacting the poetry, even if they find the sound of *Pink Thunder* foreign. And if your daily soundtrack is provided by Pavement, Neko Case, the National, or Elliott Smith, then the guitar / bass / drums trinity, the vintage keyboard sonorities, and the tightly compressed drums are going to instantly connect with your sense of all that is right in the world, while the asymmetrical forms, the non-metric passages, and the extended harmonies might introduce you to new musical dimensions.

By grounding these songs in the conventions of Indie Rock, Zapruder makes them accessible and immediate; by using art song techniques, he creates new structures and keeps the relationship between the words and music as the guiding element. So we get the pleasures of Indie Rock in expanded and inventive forms.

For example, in Bob Hicok's "Twins," there is a pause after the lines, "She is two places at once / And she is two places at once / Which is four places at once." It's a momentary break that perfectly enacts the confused addition demanded by the absurdity of the words—an agile programmatic gesture. And in the song, "Pennsylvania," we get the full sonic representational treatment of "a big fucking deal tree," introduced by a fat electric bass slide and followed by super low toms—iconic sounds of Indie Rock put to subtle use.

Zapruder writes a straightforward, gorgeous tune with a classic feel like "Storm Window," tapping into quiet domesticity ala "Our House" or "She's Leaving Home," but skewers it with the acidic literary poignancy of Mary Ruefle's "poems of mist," "blood-red leather novels," and a "three-legged white cat," adding parallel layers of meaning alongside the text through his interpretation. The album is even filled with tiny popish hooks such as the turn on the word "twilight" in Brett Fletcher Lauer's "Song," physical pleasures like the loose blown-out dance rhythms on Sierra Nelson's "Last Word," and humorous genre nods like the loping country two-step in David Berman's "Civics."

At its root, the wide-ranging music of *Pink Thunder* is dedicated to fully exploring and expressing the poetic texts with accuracy, subtlety—and ultimately—revelatory power.

I recently asked Zapruder what he saw as the use of these songs, what is their function? He said, "I want to make people have an experience of aliveness and truth and insight that is somehow philosophical or contemplative or meaningful. I believe that art can help people, put people in contact with, I guess their green and growing edge, whatever you want to call it—that part of them that feels alive: their humanity, their right to have their own experience."

Maybe this is the core of what makes Pink Thunder new? The use of these songs? Their function. If a song is something that you put into your body, a foreign compound that you intimately ingest through a physical orifice, what do you want it to do for your system? Do you want it to enhance your mood? To erase your memory? To blot out your pain? To turn you on? To make you dance around? To make the world look weird? Or make the world look less weird? To make you laugh? To put you to sleep? To keep you awake? To help you commune with strangers and loved ones? To help you memorize facts? To make you feel closer to your god? To expedite and accelerate the passage of your work day?

What if there was a song that you could put inside your body that helped you be more alive? That helped you live a more meaningful existence? That put you directly in touch with your green and growing edge?

Or perhaps more accurately, the question should be "What if there wasn't?"

Scott Pinkmountain
Pioneertown, CA – August 2012

Artist's Statement

Hello listeners and lookers,

In the Fall of 2006, I met up with the Wave Books Poetry Bus in Charlotte, North Carolina and rode along from there to New Orleans. I had been spending most of my time writing and recording songs and taking every opportunity to talk with poets and other song-writers about the relationship between songs and the written word, especially poems. I wanted to turn poems into songs to learn more about that relationship. I wanted to hear what would happen.

For about a week I rode the bus and listened to readings every night. I slept in the bus, too, and maybe my dreams mingled with the poets' because I got their music in my ear. I could hear quieter and quieter music each day, until the poets' readings became as song-like as actual songs. I had a keyboard and headphones with me, and as the bus rolled South, I sat in the back writing music and reading poems.

When I left New Orleans to go back to California, I took a folder of poems and a bunch of books home with me, and I read through them and picked poems that suggested themselves to me as song-like. I picked things by instinct. After a year or so, I had a lot of poems picked, but had only finished turning a few of them into songs. I wasn't getting enough done. So, in January of 2008 I rented a little cottage in Napa, California to hole up for ten writing days. I set up a digital piano and a minimal recording scenario, and I worked. I set myself a schedule: Alarms went off six times a day. From 9:30am – 12:30pm, from 1:30 – 4:00pm, and from 5:00 – 6:30pm, I wrote. It was hardcore, and I loved it. That is where and how I wrote most of the *Pink Thunder* pieces.

My basic process was to take a printed version of the poem and to essentially read my way through it, singing melodies and then harmonizing those. I'd develop anything that felt good. I followed whatever seemed promising or interesting as long as it seemed to be determined by the poem. My inviolable rule was that the poems must control the music and not vice-versa. I made a rule that I would never change a single word, nor would I reorder or otherwise alter any of the poems, and I stuck to that. I wrote chord symbols over the texts, and in some cases I just wrote simple note names above individual syllables so I wouldn't forget. I didn't use much notation at all, and I didn't think of this as composing. I thought of it as song writing— I strove to look at the printed poems as lead sheets without music.

Usually, I'd end up with a verse-like beginning, then some kind of transition to another section that would be somewhat (but not entirely) like the opening verse. These often, but not always, corresponded to obvious divisions of the poem as it appeared on the page. Once I had a beginning, I'd try to re-use musical elements as much as possible as the piece developed, and the chords or melodies of what might have been a "first verse" almost always return in truncated or otherwise altered form later in the pieces. Even so, I'd sometimes be forced to launch into totally new material halfway through the poem or later, and it was hard to avoid writing things that ended up seeming like random, stream-of-consciousness reactions to the poem. It's not very song-like to introduce totally new ideas late in the proceedings, and I worked hard to make sure these "deep verses," as I came to call them, were musically viable.

A few months after being in Napa, I booked time with Sean Coleman at Closer Recording in San Francisco, thinking we'd just go in and track everything and all would be good. I immediately realized that it wasn't going to be that easy, and that these were not songs like I had recorded before. Things that I had been pretty sure were compositionally solid sounded forced and improbable. Tempos that seemed right in the studio were all wrong when I listened later. I got very discouraged about the songs and the project overall. I wouldn't say I was close to giving up; but I was feeling resigned to the strong possibility that I might be making a very, very bad record. I was also worried about letting the poets down, or turning excellent poems into awful songs. Little from that first session survived to be on the final record, and most of what did survive was radically altered.

It was a full year before I wanted to even consider working on the recordings again. I called Eli Crews at New, Improved Recording in Oakland, California, and Eli and I worked on and off at his place for a year or so, and between those sessions I did a lot of work in my studio in downtown Oakland. I recorded most of the vocals at my space. These songs were very hard to sing, probably since the words didn't provide the same kind of singular point of view, or repetition, of most song lyrics. Who exactly was singing, and how could the words be communicated convincingly? It was very frustrating a lot of the time. Finally, Eli and I mixed everything at Tiny Telephone Studios in San Francisco. Then, predictably for this record, we mixed everything again at New, Improved. Finally in 2010, three and a half years after riding the Poetry Bus, *Pink Thunder* was done.

***

I started out wondering if a song can be as specific, as particular as a poem. After doing this, I think the answer is yes, but not in the way I thought it would be. Nothing can equal silence as a back-ground for communication. Silence is the full spectrum. Its power lies in its potential, which is infinite. Within that silence, these poets can achieve the ultimate, most accurate communication.

Music is specific but in a different way. It seems inevitable that music of any kind, even the most avant-garde, constructs some kind

of emotional ground, or at least elicits a primal sensual or sensory reaction from people. If this kind of sound-that-creates-a-reaction is wrapped around the words of a poem, then a certain reading of that poem—one that is more specifically contextualized than a reading conducted against silence—is made. Because there is sound where silence might be, it seems these songs can't avoid being specific interpretations of the poems. If all arts aspire to the condition of music, then the music of *Pink Thunder* aspires to, but never fully achieves the condition of silence.

My interest in this project was always more about songs than it was about poems. All along, on some level I was thinking about song, meaning singy-songy song, the common, public tree of song that grew from lullabies and work songs and things like that. It's true that there's some fancy music in *Pink Thunder*, but, after submitting to the poem, every sound on the recordings submits to that same second master: the gentle song. The question I had was: If I sang these particular poems with music happening, but tried to do that as closely as possible to what a typical reading might be, what kind of songs would emerge? Would they take on the same kind of crystalline shock of truth that the poems have? What musical forms would emerge?

Ultimately I came to think that the music of a poem is like a mobile. It is not true that these poems have no music at all. In fact, the good ones have certain shapes—rhythms, vowels and consonants, phrases—that, while they don't recur exactly, return in slight transformations. First you see them straight on, then you see them from an angle as they circle away from you. It's beautiful.

This is how the music in *Pink Thunder* tries to work. I read the poems, and I listened with my inner ear's inner ear. I didn't think. I experienced the poems and worked toward sounds and melodies that honor their inner logic and nearly silent music. I wanted to make songs from the poems' DNA and from nothing else. I wanted to make mutations.

Thanks for reading and listening. Please investigate the work these poets are doing, and the publishers who create these fantastic books. Living with their words and making songs from them changed me. I hope that they will change you, too.

Michael Zapruder
Oakland, CA — July 2012

The Poems

ILLUSTRATIONS BY ARRINGTON de DIONYSO

BOOBS ARE REAL
— DOROTHEA LASKY

THEY STOLE MY TIRES
THEY KNOCKED DOWN MY HOUSE
THEY KILLED MY FATHER
THEY CUT OFF MY FINGERS
AND I THOUGHT, "AND I DID LIKE THOSE FINGERS."

THEY PIERCED MY EYELIDS. THEY SCALPED MY BRAIN.
THEY RAN THEIR SWEATY FINGERS DOWN MY SWEATY BACK.
THEY PLAYED ME MUSIC BUT IT WASN'T MUSIC.
THEY LOVED ME AND THEN THEY DIDN'T.
SOMEWHERE IN THERE I GREW THESE ENORMOUS BOOBS.
AT SOME POINT WHAT ▓▓▓▓▓▓ THEY TOOK AWAY
WAS GIVEN BACK
IN THE FORM OF BOOBS.
WHAT THEY TOOK FROM ME
THEY GAVE BACK
JUST LIKE, AS LYDIA DAVIS SAYS,
WHEN A LIMIT HAS BEEN REACHED
WHAT IS REAL BUT DOES NOT HELP
IS LOST FOREVER AND REPLACED BY THE UNREAL.
THE DIFFERENCE IS = THESE BOOBS ARE REAL.

CHIA PET CEMETERY

D.A. POWELL

THE PLOT HAS BEEN OVERGROWN SINCE THE LAST GOOD RAIN
VISITED FRACTURED POTTERY TO THE GRAVE
JUST THE SIZE OF A POSTHOLE WILL DO: *le petit mort*

IF THERE IS A SHEET OF FOG, IT IS A FLEECE, IT IS A CIRCLING FLOCK
THE NIGHT COMES AS A FLAG OF CREPE WAVING US DOWN

Down fills the finest pillow YOU SAID, WISEACRE
WISEACRE, I SAID, BECAUSE I DIDN'T YET KNOW ITS ROOT
YOU SAID YOU'D TAKE CARE OF EVERYTHING, AS IF
THE VERY WISH TO BE AN UMBRELLA COULD EXPAND

FIRST: YOU NEED A GOOD HAIRCUT AND A SHAVE

SECOND: WHAT WERE WE GOING TO TEND IF NOT OURSELVES
NOT CHILDREN. ADOPT-A-HIGHWAY. A HOME FOR WAYWARD BEAGLES

WATER THE PLANTS, I SAID, WATER THE DAMNED PLANTS

WELL, YOU DID MANAGE TO WATER THE PLANTS

AT PLAY IN MY GARDEN ON SUNDAY MORNING

~CARRIE ST. GEORGE COMER

JUNK FLARES INSIDE ME. JUNK: IT FLARES INSIDE ME
LIKE THIS CATERPILLAR BURNING IN NEWSPAPER.
LIFE IS A RING OF RED BEADS. MY FATHER ONCE SAID THAT,
AND NOW I KNOW WHAT HE MEANT. LIFE IS A SABLE COAT,
IT DRAGS ALONG THE GROUND BEHIND US,
IT WEIGHS ON THE SHOULDERS LIKE A HUNDRED SILKY DEAD.
SHE WORE IT TO THE OPERA ONE SPRING NIGHT; THE YELLOW LIGHT
OF ENORMOUS WINDOWS BLEW THROUGH THE DARKNESS.
HERE'S THE TROUBLE WITH THE HEAVYASSEDNESS OF EVERYTHING.

IN A PINK VELOUR POCKET, A TINY SOUL STIRS. IT NEEDS TO DIE.
YOU THINK THE SOUL IS MINE, BUT NO, IT'S HERS.
SHE STARES OUT THE WINDOW, HER YOUNG EYES LIKE BITS OF DEAD MOUSE
WITH THE FEET STILL ATTACHED. SHE STARES AT THE EXACT SPOT WHERE
SOMEONE IS SMASHING HER WINDSHIELD WITH A DAY STAR.
THE DARKEST HEART ISN'T DARK AT ALL. IT IS A WHITE FLOWER.
IT UNFOLDS AND SITS ALONE IN RED RIVERS.

TWINS

BOB HICOK

SHE HAS A DREAM AND SHE HAS THE SAME DREAM.
SHE SAYS MOON AND SHE SAYS MOON AND BOTH PUT THEIR SHE-PHONES
TO THEIR CHESTS.
SHE SAYS IN MY DREAM I SLEPT BETWEEN YOUR MATTRESS AND BOXSPRING
AND SHE NODS AND SHE HEARS HER NOD.

SHE SAYS I WAS IN THE BLUE DRESS BEFORE YOU PUT IT ON
AND AFTER YOU PUT IT ON, LIKE A SOFT PAPER FLOWER SHE SAYS
AND SHE SAYS YES, LIKE A SOFT PAPER FLOWER.

SHE NESTLES THE PHONE IN HER CROTCH AND SHE NESTLES THE PHONE
IN HER CROTCH AND THE PUBIC HAIRS SAY IT WAS WARM IN THE DREAM.

SHE PUTS HER FACE AGAINST THE COOL WINDOW AND THEY PLAY
WHERE'S MY FACE AND SHE GUESSES AGAINST THE COOL WINDOW.

SHE SAYS I HUNG UP THE PHONE AN HOUR AGO AND SHE SAYS
I HUNG UP THE PHONE LAST YEAR AND STILL WE GO ON TALKING
SHE SAYS AND SHE SAYS WE GO ON TALKING EVEN WHILE I AM DEAD
AND EVEN WHEN I'M COMING BACK TO LIFE

SHE IS TWO PLACES AT ONCE AND SHE IS TWO PLACES AT ONCE
WHICH IS FOUR PLACES AT ONCE.

SHE HAS TO GO BACK TO SLEEP NOW AND SHE HAS TO GO BACK TO SLEEP NOW.

SHE SAYS ARE YOU ASLEEP NOW AND SHE SAYS YES AND ARE YOU ASLEEP NOW
AND SHE SAYS YES AND THEY GO ON TALKING ABOUT BEING ASLEEP NOW.

SHE HAS A DREAM AND SHE HAS THE SAME DREAM AND IN THE DREAM
SHE IS DREAMING WHAT SHE DREAMS AND SHE IS DREAMING WHAT SHE DREAMS.

THEN IT RAINS.

PENNSYLVANIA

-JOSHUA BECKMAN, ANTHONY McCANN,
TRAVIS NICHOLS, MATTHEW ZAPRUDER

IN THE FOREST WRITING ON A TREE

I FOUND A TREE

A NAKED TREE
A BIG FUCKING DEAL TREE

I'VE BEEN YOUR GIRLFRIEND FOR SEVERAL MINUTES
AND IT'S BEEN GRAND BUT I MUST BE GOING
TO THE STARCASE TO CLIMB A FEW
SPROCKETS OF DENVER
TO THE BALCONY OVER THESE UNBUTTONED LIGHTS

         ✶   ✶   ✶

IF I COULD SEE IT I WOULD RIP IT UP
GOODBYE, BUT DON'T FORGET THE LILIES
SWEAT-SOAKED AND FROND CROSSED
ON THE BED WE SHARED

NOW JUST A LITTLE BIT OF
WHAT **WAS**

LEFT

AND JUST A FEW MINUTES TO FIND YOUR
SHOES

WHY

THAT'S A FABULOUS IDEA

CROSSING PENNSYLVANIA SEPARATELY AND NOT MEETING UNTIL THE BORDER
WHEN I WILL PRESENT YOU TO THE AUTHORITIES
AS THE X FACTOR
AS THE SNAPPING CONUNDRUM OF THE ALLEGHENY VALLEY
AS THE SUMMIT NAMED FOR THE SHITTIEST DAY IN STATE HISTORY.

THEN   YOU   WILL   RISE   INTO THE AIR MOUTHING

OLIVE JUICE OLIVE JUICE OLIVE JUICE OLIVE JUICE

LIKE TECHNOLOGY YOU ARE LIKE TECHNOLOGY

EVERYTHING YOU DO OTHERPEOPLE WANTTODOIT TOO

OPERA

Matthew Zapruder

OPERA POURING FROM THE TENEMENT,
DARK SOBBING INTO THE LIGHT.
CALLAS DRINKING ABSINTHE
UNDER AN ASSUMED NAME
IN TOULON THEN SINGING
CALYPSO FOR SAILORS ASLEEP
IN A BASEMENT. THOSE
GREAT SONGS ARE NOT OUR SONGS.
SONGS WE KNOW CROWN US
LIKE FLOWERS. SONGS OF THE PAST
NOELLE THEIR WHITE WALLS

ALL AROUND ME RETURN
GOLD SOUNDS BIG CLEAN AMPS
ONCE CHIMED SO SAD AND TRANSISTOR,
MACHINES PLAYED DRUMS, IT WAS
THE FASHION NOW DISTANT
AND COLD ENOUGH TO TROUBLE

THE GHOST IN YOU STILL RIDING YOUR BIKE
UNDER PINK HI FIDELITY THUNDER.

7

[CALMLY GRASS BECOMES A WAVE]
-HOA NGUYEN

CALMLY GRASS BECOMES A WAVE
SEE THE BODY PARTS YOU NAME
UNSOOTHES YOU WHERE YOU SLIP
TRYING TO WRITE OR WAKE UP

THE SONGS OVERLAP EACH OTHER   BABY

AN ECHO KNELL A CREASED PIT

AN ANIMAL

AN ANIMAL

HELLO   CALL ME

FLORIDA

TRAVIS NICHOLS

WHEN I WAS A KID MY DAD TOLD ME
THE STARS MADE THE SOUND OF CRICKETS.
THE SILVER TRILLS THAT KEPT ME UP UNTIL
THEN EVERY NIGHT WEREN'T SPILLING FROM
THE LEGS OF LITTLE BLACK INSECTS BUT BRILLIANT
POINTS OF LIGHT IN THE SKY.
HE SAID THIS TO ME FROM OUTSIDE MY WINDOW IN THE
EARLY MORNING OR DEEP NIGHT IN A SLEEP VOICE
I THOUGHT WAS THE GULF OF MEXICO
FUMBLING INTO THE SHORE, SO I WHISPERED BACK,
THE OCEAN WAS A LIAR AND I KNEW IT BECAUSE THE OTHER DAY
MY DAD TOLD ME THE STARS WEREN'T SPIDER EGGS BUT
DISTANT SILENT SUNS SO FAR AWAY THEY MAY ALREADY HAVE DIED
AND ONLY THE LIGHT EXISTS OF THEM NOW
ON THE GREAT INVISIBLE NET CAST OUT BY OUR EYES,
THEN SOMETHING STRANGE HAPPENED.
HIS GIANT BALD HEAD ROSE INTO THE WINDOW FRAME FOLLOWED
BY HIS ONE GREEN EYE, ONE BLUE EYE, THEN HIS RED
VEINED NOSE AND FINALLY HIS BEARD FUZZED MOUTH
WHICH SANG OUT IN A CLEAR HUMAN VOICE
I HAVE BEEN AFRAID OF EVER SINCE.

FALL

— MATT ROHRER

THE SUN GOES DOWN BUT THE LIGHT NEVER GOES,
RAIN MOVES THROUGH THE ORANGE
NIGHT BUT DOESN'T FALL.

THE CYPRESSES SWELL LIKE EVERYTHING ELSE

IN THE WORLD AND IN THE AIR, TURNING

IN CYCLES.

WE ARE HAPPY AND THEN INEXPLICABLY SAD

THEN HAPPY AGAIN, LIKE THE CLOUDS
IN THE SKY.

RAIN SLANTS ACROSS THE YARD,
OVER THE GRAVES OF OUR LESSER PETS.
I DON'T KNOW

IF THEIR LIVES WERE MISERABLE IN THEIR LITTLE BOXES
OR IF THEY JUST LIVED,
WITHOUT NEWS OF THE WORLD,

UNTIL THEY DIED. I CAN SEE THEIR BONES
CLEARLY WHEN I THINK REALLY HARD,
THEY MAKE A PATTERN MY TRAINING HASN'T PREPARED ME

TO UNDERSTAND.

BIRDMAN

— GILLIAN CONOLEY

I FEEL THIS TRAGIC FIGURE SITTING ON ME

AS STARS DOT TO DOT OVER THE WATER THAT IS POTABLE.

AS SHOEBLACK IN THE HAIR WILL DEFOLIATE THE SCALP.

AS LYRIC, LYRIC CRIES THE VERB, SPEAKING OF THE THING.

(AS THE LAWYER LOOKS AROUND FOR AN ASHTRAY.)

THE FERRY'S ARC   THE FERRY'S LAMP

THE INCHOATE SUMAC   THE INCHOATE SUMAC'S
                                                    BLONDE WIG

TOSSED CASUALLY NOW ABOVE THE ROCKS.

CITY AS THE MERCIFUL END OF PERSPECTIVE,
CITY AS.

HE SAID   MAY WE TALK BRIEFLY SO THAT GOD
                                            CAN BE GLIMPSED

AND ALONGSIDE HUMAN CONVERSATION.

HERON. HILARITY. TIME,

HILARIOUS WHITE SPOONBILL THAT CANNOT BE HELD IN THE MIND.

EROTIC RIPPLE MARKS ON SHORE

FAILING TO PROVE ONE'S PRESENCE,
MY HALTING ATTEMPT IN THE GUSTING SPRAY.

YES, SIR. YELLOW PINE.

SOME ARE MORE RELEASED BY WORDS. FOR SOME HELL IS
                                    OTHER PEOPLE

HE WEARS A GREEN EYESHADE CAP, LIKE AN AGING UMPIRE,

IN JANUARY 1943 ISSUE OF AMERICAN CANARY

TITLE: "I WONDER."

HE SPOKE FOR THE PILLARS, THE BARS, THE SEA AIR, THE PERPENDICULAR PRONOUN,
THE LITTLE GODS RUNNING AROUND THE ROCKS WITH SMALL BLACK CAMERAS.

SOMETIMES I TOO FEEL LIKE A MOTHERLESS
SAYS THE LAWYER,

NEURAL DAMAGE, AGREES

THE DOCTOR, EACH TO EACH AND IN THEIR HORRIBLE PENMANSHIP.

AND NATURE DOES NOT ABHOR.

ONCE I WAS A HOUSE SPARROW

NOW I AM A YELLOW HAMMER

STORM WINDOW
MARY RUEFLE

SHE SAT WRITING LITTLE POEMS OF MIST
AND HE IN AN ARMCHAIR, READING
BLOOD-RED LEATHER NOVELS.
THEIR THREE-LEGGED WHITE CAT
WANDERING BETWEEN THEM,
TWENTY-FOUR CHAMPAGNE GLASSES
SPARKLING ON THE SHELF.
NEVER A ONE TO BE BROKEN
AND TWO STONE DOGS ON EITHER SIDE
OF THE DRIVEWAY.

FOR THESE REASONS
THEY HAVE GONE ON PRECISELY,
UNDETECTED, FOR CENTURIES.

THAT YOU GO ON

— JOSHUA BECKMAN

THAT YOU GO ON, THAT YOU DO IT TOO
OR ONCE HAVE DONE — TO TEAR AT THAT,
I FAIL YOUR WANT AND SWEET SOUND,
AND WATCH THEM WAIT FOR MY FAILURE.
FUTURE PEOPLE, I WENT TO THE MUSEUM
AND SAW ALL SO CURIOUS AND SUBSTANTIAL
MAKE ITS PRESENCE KNOWN ABOVE ME,
AND SO THRILLED WITH THE GIFTS
OF HUMANS I WAS, THEIR TALENTS, THAT
SOON I DEPARTED — THE COLD AND PLEASANT SUN,
THE MIDDAY, A BUSINESS IN GREAT EXCESS,
OF THE CRUELTY OF PEOPLE,
AND IN THIS AND MY OWN JOYOUS WAY
I RETURNED HOME — SOME DAY OR SO
LATER I LOOKED FROM THE SKY UPON
A WARM OCCUPANT GLOW. YOU LEARNED A
BETTER WAY, AND I FILLED
MYSELF WITH SILLY PILLS.
FOR YEARS WE FLOATED THIS WAY,
YOUR HUSBAND NEVER KNOWING. A
SMALL CIRCLE OF SALT AROUND YOUR BODY.

MY GRANDMOTHER BY VALZHYNA MORT
TRANSLATED BY THE AUTHOR AND FRANZ WRIGHT

MY GRANDMOTHER
DOESN'T KNOW PAIN
SHE BELIEVES THAT
FAMINE IS NUTRITION
POVERTY IS WEALTH
THIRST IS WATER
HER BODY IS LIKE A GRAPEVINE WINDING AROUND A WALKING
                                        STICK
  HER HAIR BEE'S WINGS
  SHE SWALLOWS THE SUN SPECKLES OF PILLS

  AND CALLS THE INTERNET A TELEPHONE TO AMERICA

  HER HEART HAS TURNED INTO A ROSE — THE ONLY THING YOU CAN DO
  IS SMELL IT
PRESSING YOURSELF TO HER CHEST
THERE'S NOTHING ELSE YOU CAN DO WITH IT
ONLY A ROSE
HER ARMS LIKE STORK'S LEGS
RED STICKS
AND I'M ON MY KNEES
HOWLING LIKE A WOLF
AT THE WHITE MOON OF YOUR SKULL

GRANDMOTHER,

I'M TELLING YOU THIS IS NOT PAIN

IT'S JUST THE EMBRACE OF A VERY STRONG GOD

ONE WITH AN UNSHAVEN CHEEK

THAT PRICKLES WHEN HE KISSES YOU

CIVICS

— DAVID BERMAN

SHE HAD BEEN THE COURT STENOGRAPHER
IN THE LITTLE VILLAGE FOR TWO DECADES
WHEN SHE DISAPPEARED INTO THE MOUNTAINS.

I WAS PART OF THE SEARCH PARTY THAT DAY.
SNOW WAS PENDING AND THE BARE BRANCHES
LOOKED LIKE MOUNTED ANTLERS ON THE CANYON WALLS.

I WALKED WITH GLEN FROM WHITE MOON INSURANCE
FOR HOURS THROUGH COLUMNS OF SHIMMERING FIRS
AND OVER PONDS FROZEN INTO OPAL TABLES

UNTIL, ARRIVING AT AN OVERLOOK AT DUSK,
WE HEARD THE CRACKING OF A HAMMER
ECHOING THROUGH THE BURNISHED VALLEY
AND SAW WHAT LOOKED LIKE THE OLD JUDGE
AND TWELVE OTHER MEN AND WOMEN
PITCHING CAMP FOR THE NIGHT.

WORD

—JOE WENDEROTH

WE'LL BEGIN WITH WHAT'S IRREPLACEABLE.

IF YOU HAVE ONE PHOTOGRAPH, FOR INSTANCE,

OF SOMEONE YOU LOVED,

SOMEONE WHO'S GONE NOW—

WE'LL BEGIN WITH THAT.

PUT IT IN THE FIRE.

ISN'T IT LIKE FELLING

—AT ONCE—

A WHOLE HERD?

WHEN THE DUST HAS SETTLED,

YOU FEEL LIKE YOU SHOULD SAY A FEW WORDS,

DON'T YOU?

ALL THE WORDS

BEGIN TO FALL

AND YOU WILL NOT LIVE

TO HEAR THEIR DUST

SETTLED.

JOHN LOMAN: I WORK WITH NEGROES
-TYEHIMBA JESS

I HAVE BEEN ASKED: WHY DID YOU CHOOSE TO WORK
WITH THE NEGRO? CALL ME LIBRARIAN—
IN-THE-STACKS-OF-ALMOST-LOST-MELODY.
I JOURNEY THIS COLOSSAL, QUAKING BOOK.

THEY'VE AUTHORED IN THE SPACE BETWEEN THEIR LEGS,
OVER BLIND FOOL HEARTS, BENEATH STOMPING FEET,
IN THE LIQUID ENGINE OF THEIR CROONED BREATH.
AND SOMETIMES, THE SPLINTERED EDGES OF VOICE

ROOT ME IN THEIR TREE OF SINGING SUNLIGHT,
TAKE ME BACK TO SOMETHING THAT DOESN'T HAVE
A NAME; **OUR BURIED SENSE**, A BURNING WE LOST
ALONG THE WAY TO CIVILIZATION.

FROM AN ISLAND

James Tate

FOGGED IN ALL DAY, THE LONG, LOW HORNS ANNOUNCING
THE PASSING OF ANOTHER GHOSTSHIP.
BUT WE SEE NOTHING. IT'S AS IF A CURTAIN HAD BEEN DROPPED.
GO BACK INTO YOURSELF, IT SAYS, NONE OF THIS MATTERS
TO YOU ANYMORE. ALL THAT DRAMA, COLOR, MOVEMENT—
YOU CAN LIVE WITHOUT IT. IT WAS AN ILLUSION,
A TEASE, A LIE. THERE IS NOTHING OUT HERE BUT SMOKE

FROM THE RUBBLE THAT WAS EVERYTHING,
EVERYTHING YOU WANTED, EVERYTHING YOU THOUGHT
YOU NEEDED. SHIPS PASSING, FORGET IT.
CHILDREN BATHING, THERE'S NO SUCH THING.

LET GO, YOUR ISLAND IS A MOTE OF DUST.
BUT THE HORNS OF THE GHOSTSHIP SAY, REMEMBER US,
WE REMEMBER YOU.

(LAST WORDS) — SIERRA NELSON

SO LONG, SEE YOU SAILOR.
IT MAY NOT BE NEW, BUT IT'S NEW FOR
HER

PUT THIS APPLE IN YOUR POCKET,
CALL ME WHEN YOU GET THERE

THE FLOWERS ARE BLOOMING IN THE HIGHWAY MERIDIAN.
EVERYWHERE I LOOK, I SEE THINGS YOU
WOULD HAVE LIKED TO TAKE A PICTURE OF.
I SHUTTER MY EYES, BUT IT COMES OUT BLURRY.

I ATE ALL YOUR FAVORITE CANDIES,
BUT LEFT THE WRAPPERS IN THE BOWL
YOU MIGHT NOT HAVE NOTICED
BUT THE SUITCASES ARE DOWN
FROM THE ATTIC.
THE PAINT PEELS FROM THE CEILING
IN MEANINGFUL PATTERNS

LAST CALLS
SIGN MY CAST
HIDDEN HIP FLASK
ASK ME ANYTHING

UNDER THE EMPTY
STADIUM SEATING
DOES EVERY CITY
HAVE A ROOSEVELT HIGH?
SHE HIKED UP HER KNEE SOCKS

BLUE JACKET BLUE KISS GOOD
BY THE SEASHORE
HUDDLED AND COLD
BY THE WAY
TOOK ME 12 YEARS TO GET CORRECT POSTAGE
BY THE WAY SHE
COULDN'T
SAY IT
I JUST MEANT TO TELL YOU
STATIC ON THE LINE.
HOLARCTIC BLUE COPPERS
CUT UP THE SKY

BROTHER POEM NUMBER ONE

-JOSHUA BECKMAN, ANTHONY McCANN,
TRAVIS NICHOLS, MATTHEW ZAPRUDER

SOME WRONG TURNS YOU MAKE

GET YOU SOMEWHERE BLANK, LIKE A PARKING LOT

OUTSIDE A STADIUM

THE LEAVES BARKING

I HAD A TROUBLE IN MY NATURE

I PACED THE SUNLIGHT AT MY BORDERS

STILL THE CRUMPLED CITY SLEPT

I AM WRITING THIS FOR YOU BECAUSE I THINK YOUR MUSIC

HAS A TRAVELING NATURE

AND I AM ——— RIGHT NOW TRAVELING THROUGH

MY FRIENDS ALSO HAVE SHADOWS

THERE'S VERY LITTLE COMPLAINING

AND WE SUCK UP LOVE EVERYWHERE WE GO

HOW DO I GET TO THE SWIMMING POOL

WHERE I CAN SHAVE THE MOSS FROM MY BLOOD?

NO ONE TRAILS.

NO ONE TALKS.

ONLY THE CAROUSING MERCHANTS CAN TELL ME WHAT TO DO.

AND SO THEY WILL WHILE

I CONSIDER OTHER THINGS ABOUT YOUR NATURE

THIS WAS WRITTEN BY SEVERAL MEN

TODAY WE HAVE TO SORT OUT OUR BLOOD

CONSIDER THE ARTIFICIAL CREEK

MAKING THE ARTIFICIAL HOUSES SEEM A LOT MORE REAL

FOR A CHINESE POET WRITING THROUGH THE NIGHT UP ON THE EDGE OF MT. POLLUX

-DARA WIER

NOW I COULD SEE I'D BEEN STIRRING THE POT
FOR ALMOST TEN THOUSAND YEARS.
I COULD SEE I'D BE STIRRING FOREVER.
SO FAR NOTHING HAD CHANGED.
NOBODY APPEARED.
I STIRRED MYSELF INTO A BOTTOMLESS SLEEP,
I WAS THE SMALLEST THING IN THE WORLD,
FRAGMENT OF SPIT, RUMOR OF MUD,
SOMETHING THAT ALMOST MIGHT HAVE BEEN.
I NO LONGER HAD SKIN OR FINE HAIRS ALONG
MY ARMS FOR WIND TO CHILL OR AN ANT TO WANDER
OVER. I NO LONGER HAD FRIENDS.
NO SISTER, NO BROTHER.
I HADN'T CRIED WHEN MY FATHER & MY MOTHER
WAVED GOODBYE AND THEIR SHIP EXITED THE HARBOR.
I HADN'T ASKED THEM WHERE THEY WERE GOING
THEY LEFT ME NO INSTRUCTIONS.

SONG

— BRETT FLETCHER LAUER

BEFORE OPIUM THAT SOUL-SICK SUMMER,
AGELESS AND ALONE, INFINITE JUNE NINETEEN
NINETY NINE HOLDS TO MY MASTER. SADNESS
ARRIVED LIKE AN EMPTY CHEVROLET.
I HAVE TERRIBLE SYMBOLS. SYMBOLS THAT COME
IN SLEEP BEGINNING TO INTERRUPT, COME
DESIRING TO SPEAK WITH ME DOWNTOWN.
A HEART AS FILLED AS PERSIA WITH TWILIGHT.
DEATH STOPS DEATH, STRANGERS WHO ENVY.
LYDIA, ASK THE GODS TO EXTRUDE US.
ONLY GODS GRANT GESTURES THAT DESTROY.
ASHEN WAVES OF AUTUMN, ABSTRACT YOUR
BEING INTO A SILENT SHIP, SAILS QUIETLY FULL
OF WIND TRAVELING TO LISBON. LISTLESSLY
THOUGHTS TUMBLE THROUGH THE STREET,
AUDIBLE AS FALLEN LEAVES. THERE IS SICKNESSES
LIKE A SKY'S BLUENESS, A QUIET BOY INSIDE
A CHURCH. RAIN MYSTERIOUSLY SUDDEN

BOOK OF LIFE

—NOELLE KOCOT

THE PHOENIX ROSE FROM THE ASHES
AND DECIDED TO KEEP RISING.
A FORGETFUL MONK BASKED IN ITS SHADOW.
"BANANAS TASTE EXPENSIVE!" EXCLAIMED
THE MONK, TO NO ONE IN PARTICULAR.
SUDDENLY, THE PHOENIX SWOOPED DOWN
AND LANDED ON TOP OF HIS HEAD.
"I AM NO LONGER WEDDED TO EROS,"
THE PHOENIX WARBLED, "AND I'D LIKE
TO LIVE WITH YOU IN THE MONASTERY,
THOUGH MY WINGS ARE STILL SINGED
AND I ONLY EAT LIVE THINGS."
THE MONK RIFLED THROUGH HIS ▬ POWERPACK
AND PULLED OUT A SQUIRMING WORM.
"HERE YOU GO, MY FIERY FRIEND,
TAKE IT AND EAT IT, AND DO NOT WORRY
ABOUT THE OTHER MONKS, THEY
MEAN NO HARM. YOU ARE TO GO BACK
TO THE MONASTERY WITH ME."

THE PHOENIX FLAPPED ITS WINGS
WITH HAPPINESS. BUT SEEMINGLY
OUT OF NOWHERE, THE PHOENIX
DRILLED A HOLE IN THE GROUND WITH ITS BEAK
AND DESCENDED INTO THE CORE OF THE EARTH.
THE MONK WAS SAD AND ALONE,
BUT SINCE HE WAS FORGETFUL,
THE MEMORY OF THE PHOENIX SOON FADED.
HE HUMMED "THE LION SLEEPS TONIGHT"
ON HIS WAY BACK TO THE OTHER MONKS,
WITH A DIM RECOLLECTION OF HIS
YOUNGER YEARS, WHEN EROS LORDED

OVER HIM, AND HE WAS HAPPY.
WHEN HE RETURNED TO THE MONASTERY
HE DIED OF A FATALLY BROKEN HEART
NOT REMEMBERING EXACTLY WHY.

Boobs Are Real

Poem by Dorothea Lasky, from *Awe*, Wave Books 2007. Used with permission. Music by Michael Zapruder.

Piano, electric bass, synth bass (Hammond Piper Autochord), synthetic warbles (Juno 106), and background and lead vocals — Michael Zapruder

Piano, basses, and vocals recorded by Michael Zapruder at 1924 Franklin. Warbly synths recorded by Eli Crews at New, Improved Recording (N,IR). Mixed by Eli Crews at N,IR. Mastered by Dave McNair at Sterling Sound.

Chia Pet Cemetery

Poem by D. A. Powell, from *Chronic*, Graywolf Press 2009. Used with permission. Music by Michael Zapruder.

Acoustic guitars, electric guitars, and background and lead vocals — Michael Zapruder

Electric guitars and vocals recorded by Michael Zapruder at 1924 Franklin. Acoustic guitars recorded by Eli Crews at N,IR. Mixed by Eli Crews at N,IR. Mastered by Dave McNair at Sterling Sound.

At Play in My Garden on a Sunday Morning

Poem by Carrie St. George Comer. Used with permission. Music by Michael Zapruder.

Drums — Darian Gray
Electric bass, acoustic guitars, apps (Beatmaker, Sruti Box, Music Box), and background and lead vocals — Michael Zapruder

Bass, guitars, synthetics, and vocals recorded by Michael Zapruder at 1924 Franklin. Drums recorded by Eli Crews at N,IR. Mixed by Eli Crews at N,IR. Mastered by Dave McNair at Sterling Sound.

Twins

Poem by Bob Hicok, from *This Clumsy Living*, University of Pittsburgh Press 2007. Used with permission. Music by Michael Zapruder.

Glockenspiel, jingles and coins, organ bass, organ — Kevin Seal
Ukulele, acoustic guitar, high organs (Hammond Piper Autochord), digital squelch, and background and lead vocals — Michael Zapruder

Glockenspiel, jingles and coins, organ bass, organ, and ukulele recorded by Sean Coleman at Closer Recording. Acoustic guitar, high organs, digital squelch, and vocals recorded by Michael Zapruder at 1924 Franklin. Mixed by Eli Crews at N,IR. Mastered by Dave McNair at Sterling Sound.

Pennsylvania

Poem by Joshua Beckmann, Anthony McCann, Travis Nichols, Matthew Zapruder (written on the Poetry Bus). Used with permission. Music by Michael Zapruder.

Cello — Beth Vandervennet
Drums — Tyler Corelitz
English Horn — Kyle Bruckmann
Flute — Evan Francis
Piano — Steve Hogan
Violin — Alan Lin
Electric bass, acoustic and electric guitars, and background and lead vocals — Michael Zapruder

Cello, English horn, flute and violin recorded by Sean Coleman at Closer Recording. Drums recorded by Eli Crews at N,IR. Electric bass, acoustic and electric guitars, and vocals recorded by Michael Zapruder at 1924 Franklin. Mixed by Eli Crews at N,IR. Mastered by Dave McNair at Sterling Sound.

Opera

Poem by Matthew Zapruder, from *The Pajamaist*, Copper Canyon Press 2006. Used with permission. Music by Michael Zapruder except choral vocal arrangement by Michael Kaulkin.

Acoustic Bass — Nate Brenner
Choral vocals by members of the Pacific Mozart Ensemble: Lynne Morrow, Lark Coryell, Angie Doctor
Piano, organ, percussion, and lead vocal — Michael Zapruder

Choral vocals recorded by Eli Crews at Tiny Telephone Studios. Acoustic bass and piano recorded by Eli Crews at N,IR. Organ, percussion, and lead vocal recorded by Michael Zapruder at 1924 Franklin.

Calmly Grass Becomes a Wave

Poem by Hoa Nguyen, from *Isn't It Romantic: 100 Love Poems*, Verse Press 2004. Used with permission. Music by Michael Zapruder.

Acoustic guitars, and background and lead vocals — Michael Zapruder

Rhythm acoustic guitar recorded by Eli Crews at N,IR. Acoustic guitar lines, and vocals recorded by Michael Zapruder at 1924 Franklin. Mixed by Eli Crews at N,IR. Mastered by Dave McNair at Sterling Sound.

Florida

Poem by Travis Nichols, from *See Me Improving*, Copper Canyon Press 2010. Used with permission. Music by Michael Zapruder.

Electric bass — Nate Brenner
Drums — Tyler Corelitz
Piano — Steve Hogan
Acoustic and electric guitars, Farfisa, and background and lead vocals — Michael Zapruder

Drums, bass, and some electric guitars recorded by Eli Crews at N,IR. Piano, acoustic and some electric guitars, farfisa, and vocals recorded by Michael Zapruder at 1924 Franklin. Mixed by Eli Crews at N,IR. Mastered by Dave McNair at Sterling Sound.

Fall

Poem by Matthew Rohrer, from *Satellite*, Verse Press 2001. Used with permission. Music by Michael Zapruder.

Clarinet — Evan Francis
Cornet — Gene V. Baker
Piano, acoustic guitar, and lead vocal — Michael Zapruder

Acoustic guitar, and piano recorded by Sean Coleman at Closer Recording. Clarinet and cornet recorded by Eli Crews at N,IR. Vocals recorded by Michael Zapruder at 1924 Franklin. Mixed by Eli Crews at N,IR. Mastered by Dave McNair at Sterling Sound.

Birdman

Poem by Gillian Conoley, from *Profane Halo*, Verse Press 2005. Used with permission. Music by Michael Zapruder.

Electric guitar — Ava Mendoza
Organ bass — Gene V. Baker
Marimba — Shayna Dunkelman
Synthesizer 1 (Orchestron) — Matt Cunitz
Synthesizer 2 (Rogue), additional synths — Steve Hogan
Shaker, piano, and background and lead vocals — Michael Zapruder

Electric guitar, organ bass, marimba, and synthesizers 1 and 2 recorded by Eli Crews at Tiny Telephone Studios. Additional sythesizers recorded by Eli Crews at N,IR. Shaker, piano, and vocals recorded by Michael Zapruder at 1924 Franklin. Mixed by Eli Crews at N,IR. Mastered by Dave McNair at Sterling Sound.

Storm Window

Poem by Mary Ruefle, from *Selected Poems*, Wave Books 2010. Used with permission. Music by Michael Zapruder.

Cello — Beth Vandervennet
Electric bass — Mark Allen-Piccolo
Flute — Evan Francis
Wurlitzer — Steve Hogan
Piano and vocals — Michael Zapruder

Everything recorded by Eli Crews at N,IR except vocals, recorded by Michael Zapruder at 1924 Franklin. Mixed by Eli Crews at N,IR. Mastered by Dave McNair at Sterling Sound.

That You Go On

Poem by Joshua Beckman. Used with permission. Music by Michael Zapruder, except cello/saxophones arrangement by Michael Kaulkin.

Acoustic bass — Nate Brenner
Alto saxophones — Georgiana Krieger
Cello — Beth Vandervennet
Drums — Darian Gray
Piano and vocals — Michael Zapruder

Everything recorded by Eli Crews at N,IR except vocals, recorded by Michael Zapruder at 1924 Franklin. Mixed by Eli Crews at N,IR. Mastered by Dave McNair at Sterling Sound.

My Grandmother

Poem by Valzhyna Mort, from *Factory of Tears*, Copper Canyon Press 2008. Used with permission. Music by Michael Zapruder.

Drums — Chris McGrew
Piano — Steve Hogan
Bass, guitars, synthetic mallets and bassoon, organ, synthesizer, and background and lead vocals — Michael Zapruder

Drums and piano recorded by Sean Coleman at Closer Recording. Guitars, synthesizer, and various sonic treatments recorded by Eli Crews at N,IR. Bass, synthetic mallets, bassoon, organ, and vocals recorded by Michael Zapruder at 1924 Franklin. Mixed by Eli Crews at N,IR. Mastered by Dave McNair at Sterling Sound.

Civics

Poem by David Berman, from *Actual Air*, Open City 1999. Used with permission. Music by Michael Zapruder.

Drums — Tyler Corelitz
Electric bass — Nate Brenner
Piano — Steve Hogan
Guitars, apps (Steel Guitar), and background and lead vocals — Michael Zapruder

Everything recorded by Eli Crews at N,IR except synthetic steel guitar and vocals, recorded by Michael Zapruder at 1924 Franklin. Mixed by Eli Crews at N,IR. Mastered by Dave McNair at Sterling Sound.

Word

Poem by Joe Wenderoth, from *No Real Light*, Wave Books 2007. Used with permission. Music by Michael Zapruder.

Acoustic bass — Nate Brenner
Background vocals — Melody Parker
Drums — Darian Gray
Flute — Evan Francis
Electric guitars, piano, organ, background and lead vocals — Michael Zapruder

Bass, flute, and piano recorded by Sean Coleman at Closer Recording. Drums and background vocals recorded by Eli Crews at N,IR. Electric guitars, organ, and vocals recorded by Michael Zapruder at 1924 Franklin. Mixed by Eli Crews at N,IR. Mastered by Dave McNair at Sterling Sound.

John Lomax: I Work with Negroes

Poem by Tyehimba Jess, from *Leadbelly*, Verse Press 2005. Used with permission. Music by Michael Zapruder, except choral vocal arrangement by Michael Kaulkin and Michael Zapruder.

Choral vocals by members of the Pacific Mozart Ensemble: Dale Engle, Jeff Watts, John Paddock, and Doug Boyd
Cello — Beth Vandervennet
Violins 1 and 2 — Alan Lin
Piano — Steve Hogan
Prepared piano, and background and lead vocals — Michael Zapruder

Piano, cello, and violins recorded by Sean Coleman at Closer Recording. Prepared piano recorded by Eli Crews at N,IR. Choral vocals recorded by Eli Crews at Tiny Telephone Studios. Other vocals recorded by Michael Zapruder at 1924 Franklin. Mixed by Eli Crews at N,IR. Mastered by Dave McNair at Sterling Sound.

From an Island

Poem by James Tate, from *Worshipful Company of Fletchers*, Ecco 1994. Used with permission. Music by Michael Zapruder.

Acoustic Bass — Kurt Kotheimer
Cornets — Gene V. Baker
Celeste, piano, and vocals — Michael Zapruder

Bass and piano recorded by Sean Coleman at Closer Recording. Cornets recorded by Eli Crews at N,IR. Celeste and vocal recorded by Michael Zapruder at 1924 Franklin. Mixed by Eli Crews at N,IR. Mastered by Dave McNair at Sterling Sound.

Last Words

Poem by Sierra Nelson (written on Poetry Bus). Used by permission. Music by Michael Zapruder.

Drums — Tyler Corelitz
Bass — Nate Brenner
Choral vocals — Melody Parker
Piano, apps (Ellatron, Tongue Drum, iXylophone Pro), light bulb, and lead vocals — Michael Zapruder

Drums, bass, and choral vocals recorded by Eli Crews at N,IR. Piano, apps, light bulb, and lead vocals recorded by Michael Zapruder at 1924 Franklin. Mixed by Eli Crews at N,IR. Mastered by Dave McNair at Sterling Sound.

Brother Poem Number One

Poem by Joshua Beckmann, Anthony McCann, Travis Nichols, Matthew Zapruder (written on the Poetry Bus). Used with permission. Music by Michael Zapruder.

Background vocals, clapping — Ryan Browne, Jem Fanvu, Steve Hogan, Jed Holtzman, Kevin Seal, Michelle Solomon, Jessica Zapruder, Michael Zapruder, and Levi Zapruder
Acoustic guitar, Farfisa, Wurlitzer, bass drum, and background and lead vocals — Michael Zapruder

Wurlitzer recorded by Sean Coleman at Closer Recording. Everything else recorded by Michael Zapruder at 1924 Franklin. Mixed by Eli Crews at N,IR. Mastered by Dave McNair at Sterling Sound.

For a Chinese Poet Writing Through the Night Up on Mt. Pollux

Poem by Dara Wier, from *Remnants of Hannah*, Wave Books 2006. Used with permission. Music by Michael Zapruder.

Cello — Beth Vandervennet
English Horn — Kyle Bruckmann
Acoustic guitar, piano, synthesizer (Paraphonic 505), background and lead vocals — Michael Zapruder

Cello, English horn, and piano recorded by Sean Coleman at Closer Recording. Synthesizer recorded by Eli Crews at N,IR. Acoustic guitar and vocals recorded by Michael Zapruder at 1924 Franklin. Mixed by Eli Crews at N,IR. Mastered by Dave McNair at Sterling Sound.

Song

Poem by Brett Fletcher Lauer. Used with permission. Music by Michael Zapruder except choral vocal arrangement by Michael Kaulkin.

Cello — Beth Vandervennet
Choral vocals by members of the Pacific Mozart Ensemble: Lynne Morrow, Lark Coryell, and Angie Doctor
English horn — Kyle Bruckmann
Flute — Evan Francis
Acoustic guitars, piano, synthesizers, shaker, tambourine, and background and lead vocals — Michael Zapruder

Cello, English horn, flute, and piano recorded by Sean Coleman at Closer Recording. Synthesizers recorded by Eli Crews at N,IR. Choral vocals recorded by Eli Crews at Tiny Telephone Studios. Acoustic guitars, shaker, tambourine, and vocals recorded by Michael Zapruder at 1924 Franklin. Mixed by Eli Crews at N,IR. Mastered by Dave McNair at Sterling Sound.

Book of Life

Poem by Noelle Kocot, from *The Bigger World*, Wave Books 2011. Used with permission.
Music by Michael Zapruder.

Acoustic bass — Kurt Kotheimer
Cello — Beth Vandervennet
Drums 1 — Darian Gray
Drums 2 — Chris McGrew
Piano   Steve Hogan
Electric bass, electric guitars, tambourine, and vocals — Michael Zapruder

Acoustic bass, cello, flute, and drums 2 recorded by Sean Coleman at Closer Recording.
Drums 1 recorded by Eli Crews at N,IR. Electric bass, electric guitars, tambourine, and vocals
recorded by Michael Zapruder at 1924 Franklin. Mixed by Eli Crews at N,IR. Mastered by
Dave McNair at Sterling Sound.

Acknowledgments

Thank you to all the musicians and engineers who allowed this to happen. Special thanks to Eli Crews for heroics. Thank you to Matthew Zapruder, Joshua Beckman and Travis Nichols for the Poetry Bus. Thank you to Jesse Nathan and Dominic Luxford for believing. Thank you to Mike Fink and Douglas Smith for also believing. Thank you Janaka Stucky for true generosity, dedication and partnership, and to Carrie Olivia Adams for angelics. Thank you Dave Kostiner for protection. Thank you to the generous publishers who let these words be as free as they want to be. Thank you poets for letting me live in your words and listen there for new music. Thank you Mark Allen-Piccolo for redeeming the dream of the portmanteaus with actual electronic circuitry. Thank you Jon Bernson, Jen Welsh, and Colin Held for Transmitting. Thank you Matt Hart and Jen Woods for early support. Thank you Scott Pinkmountain for living in the territory I've worked my whole life to find. Thank you Monica Fambrough for the best ideas, always. Thank you Matthew (again) for helping me see what really matters. Thank you Alex as always for coming here with me. Thank you Mom (and Dad, in absentia) for generosity in various morphologies. Thank you Jesse Pollock, and Derek Fagerstrom and Lauren Smith at the Curiosity Shoppe, for making me something new. Thank you Jessica, for everything. Thank you Levi and Sam for arriving. Thank you listeners and readers for your beautiful and human curiosity.